EKPHRASTIC WRITING WORKBOOK

BY

MARILYN HOPE LAKE, PH.D.

ILLUSTRATED BY

MARILYN HOPE LAKE

AND DENTON WARN

ISBN-13: **978-1530421329**
ISBN-10: **1530421322**

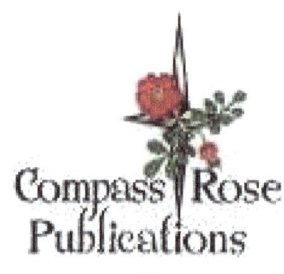

Compass Rose
Publications

For Denton,

Husband, illustrator, friend,
And last love of my life

TABLE OF CONTENTS

INTRODUCTION

The Merriam Webster Dictionary defines "ekphrasis" as a literary description of or commentary on a visual work of art. This workbook provides the writer with 20 original visual works of art intended to stimulate his or her muse—paintings, drawings, and photographs.

When you look at one of the paintings, drawings or photos, what does it bring to your writer's mind? What are your first thoughts?

Does the illustration evoke a feeling? Memory? A particular time? Poetry or prose? A sonnet? A simple verse? Flash Fiction or an anecdote? Does it call for a narrative poem? Or a short story? Perhaps a bit of whimsy?

This workbook is intended to motivate, inspire and entertain the creative spirit. It has no "how to" instructions, simply visual art and space to begin writing.

Marilyn Hope Lake
30 June 2016

PAINTINGS AND DRAWINGS

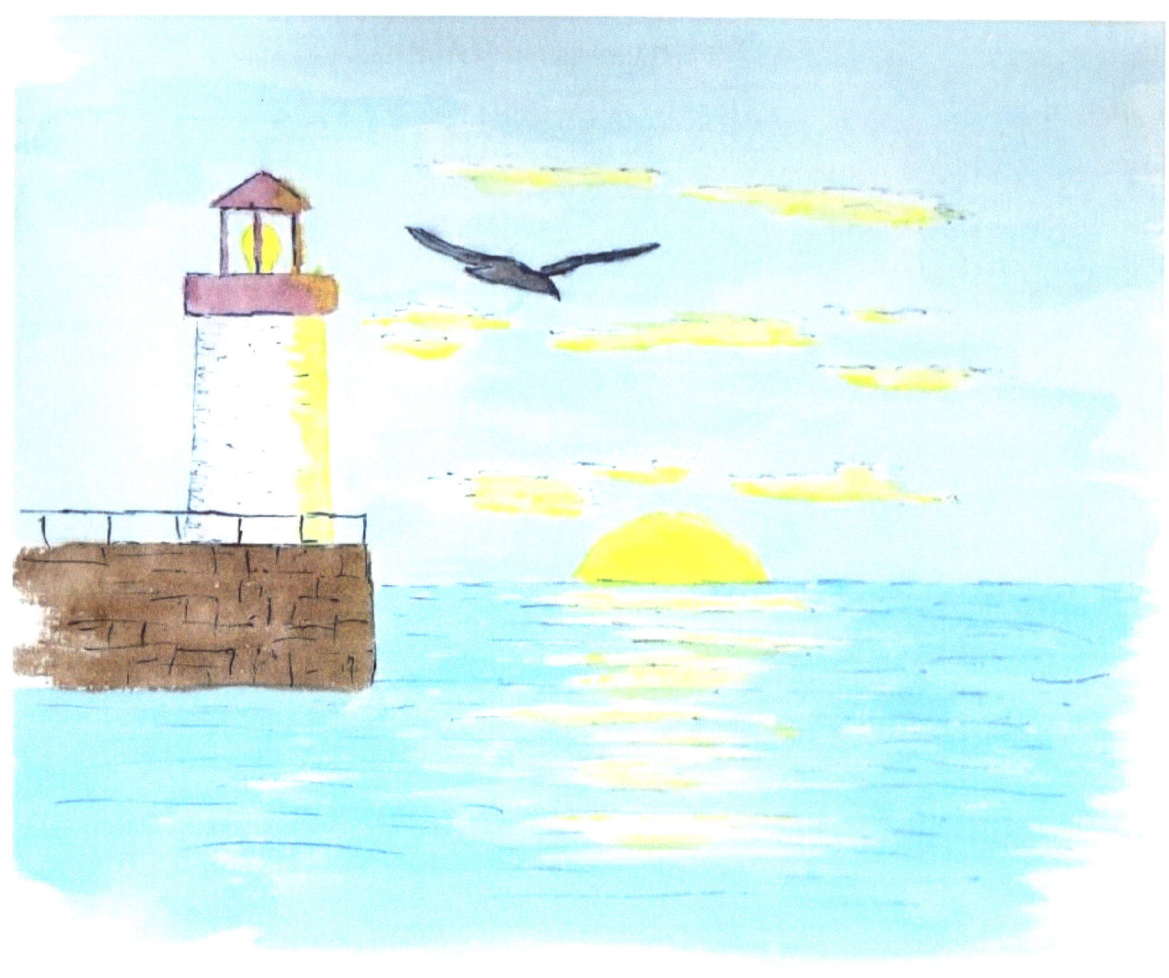

Exercise 1

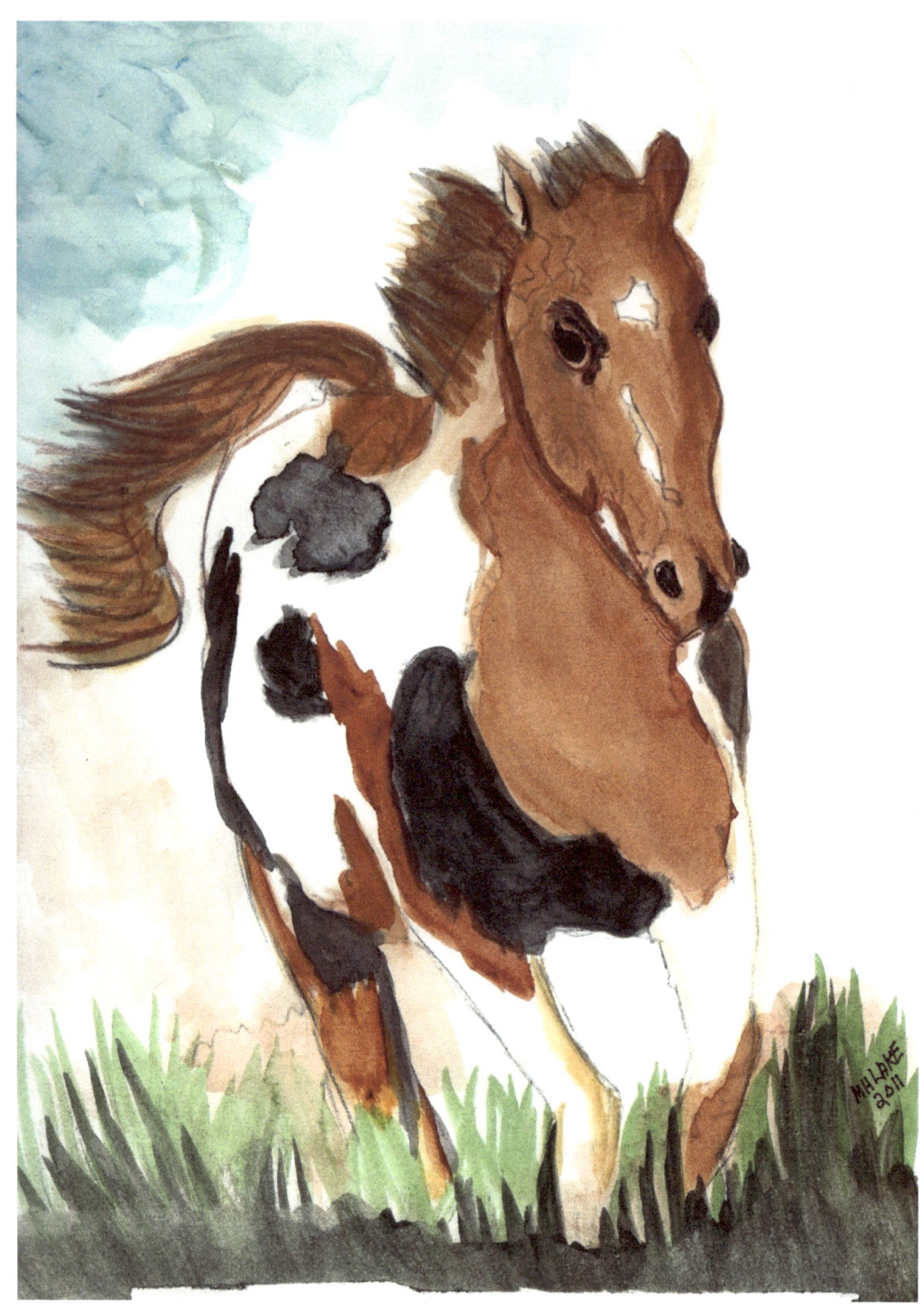

© 2011 MHLAKE

Exercise 2

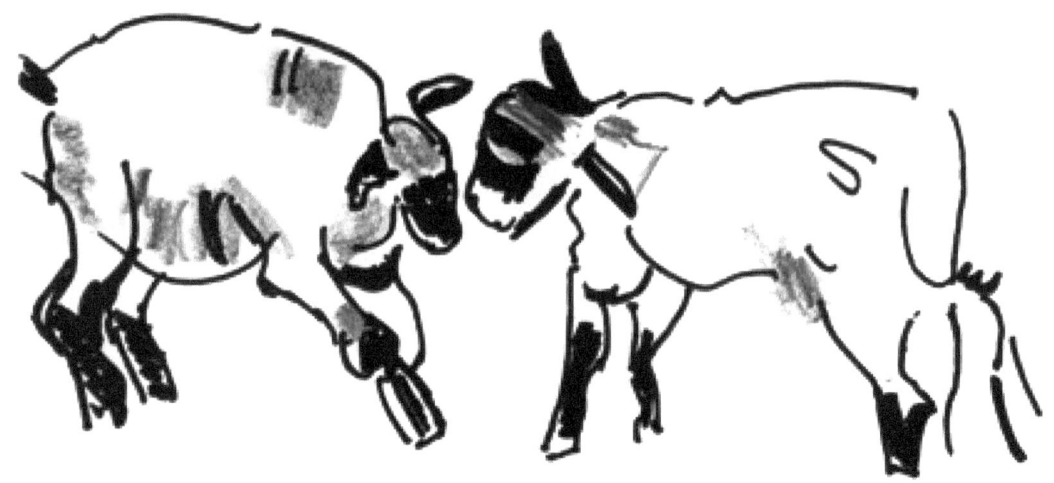

Exercise 3

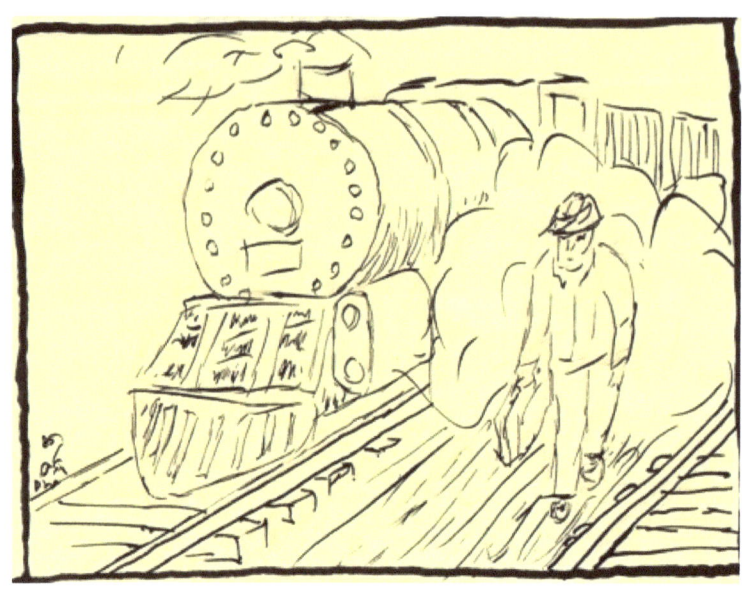

©2016 Denton Warn

Exercise 4

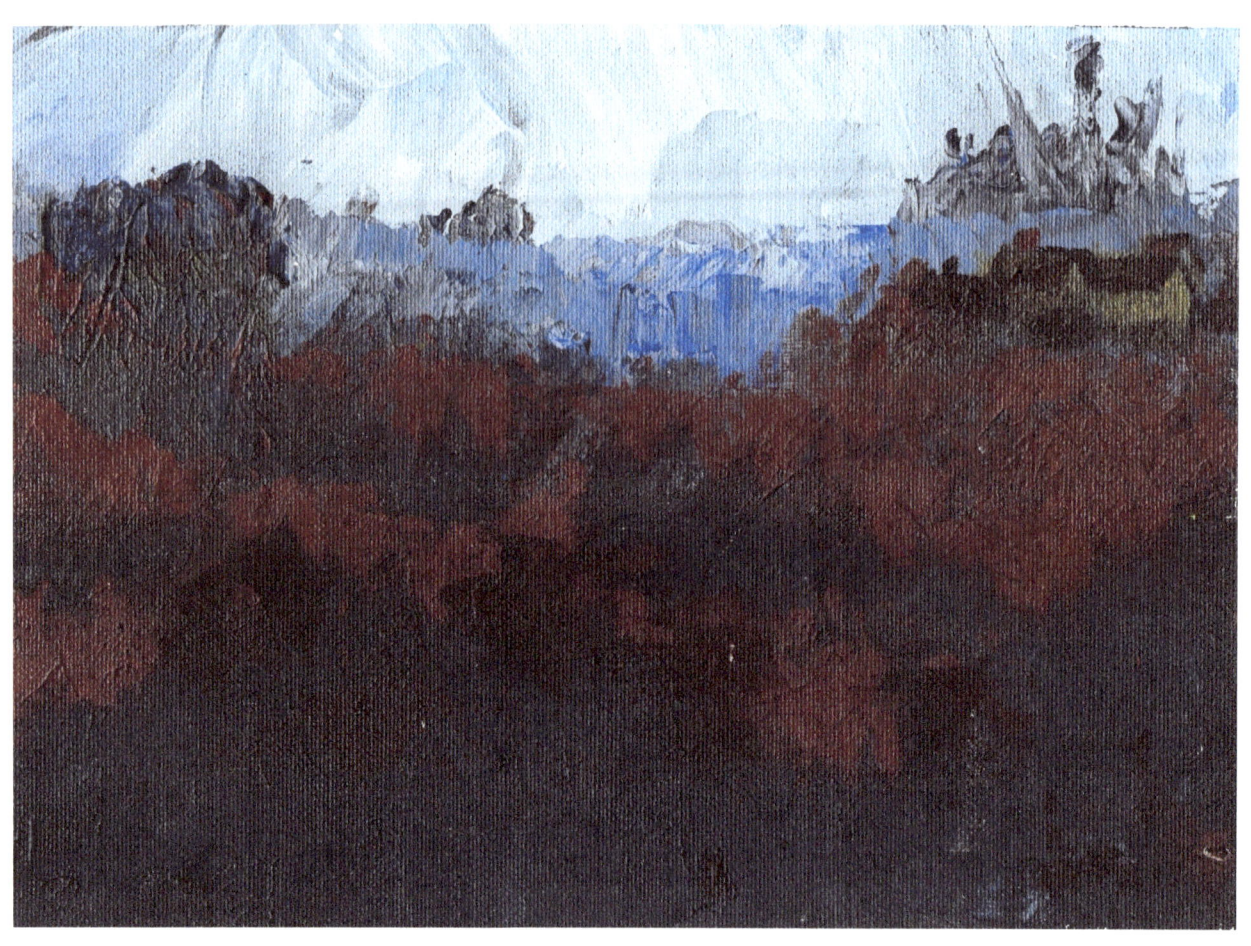

Exercise 5

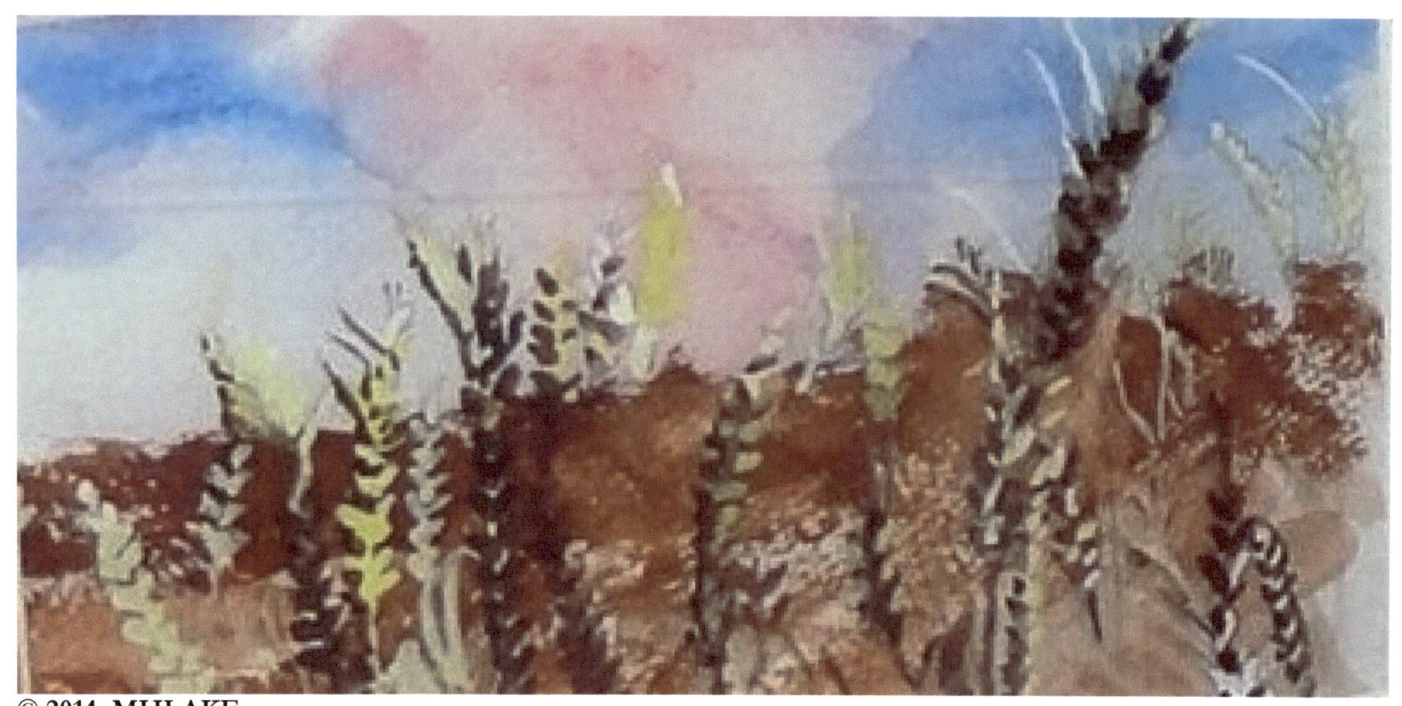

Exercise 6

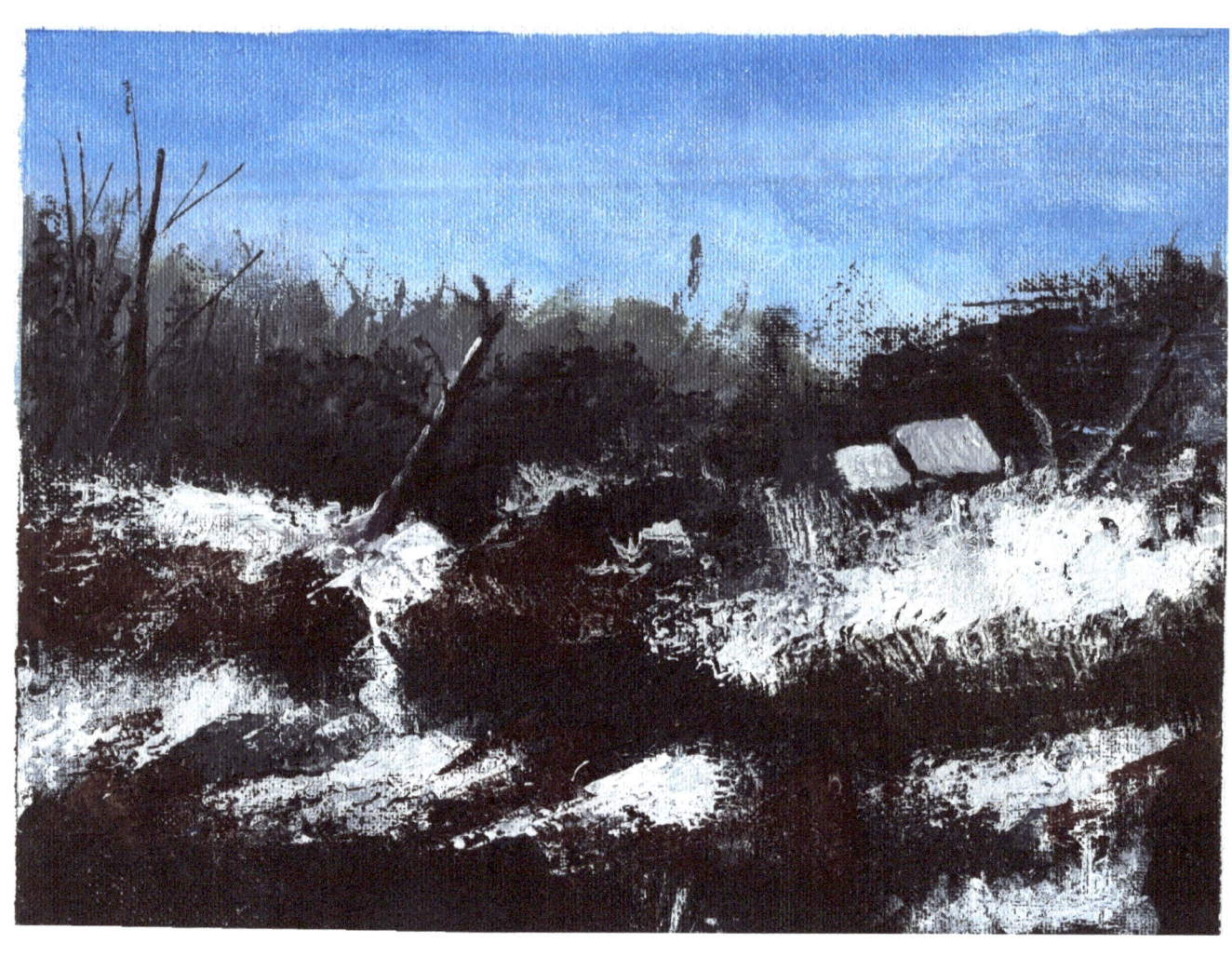

Exercise 7

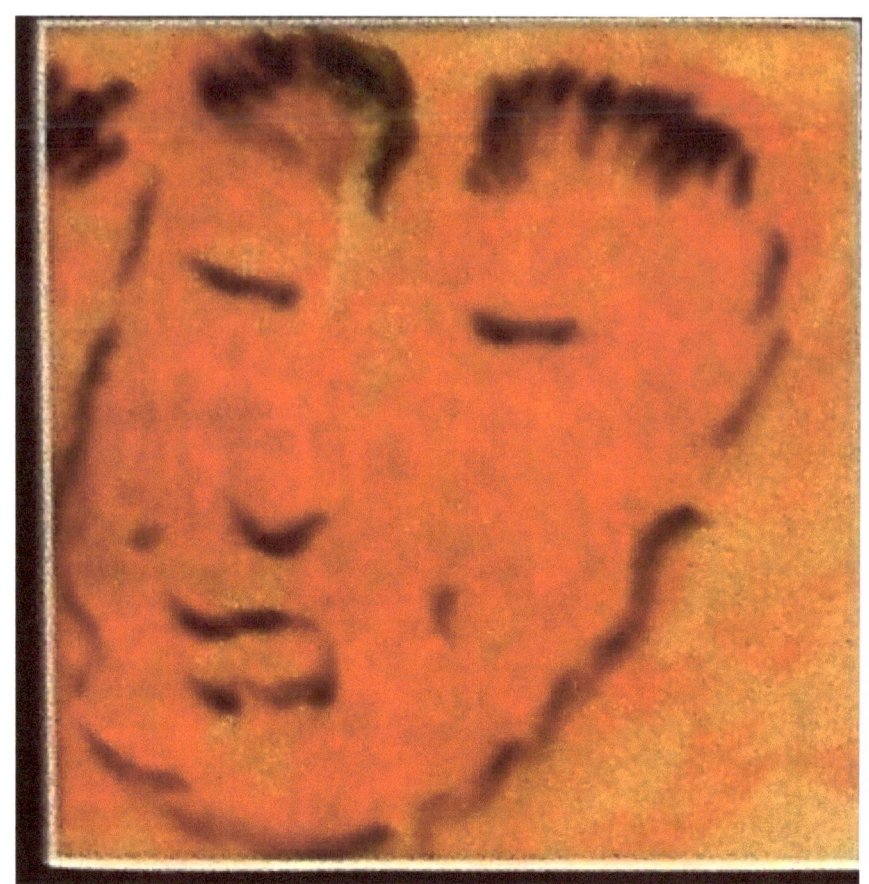

Exercise 8

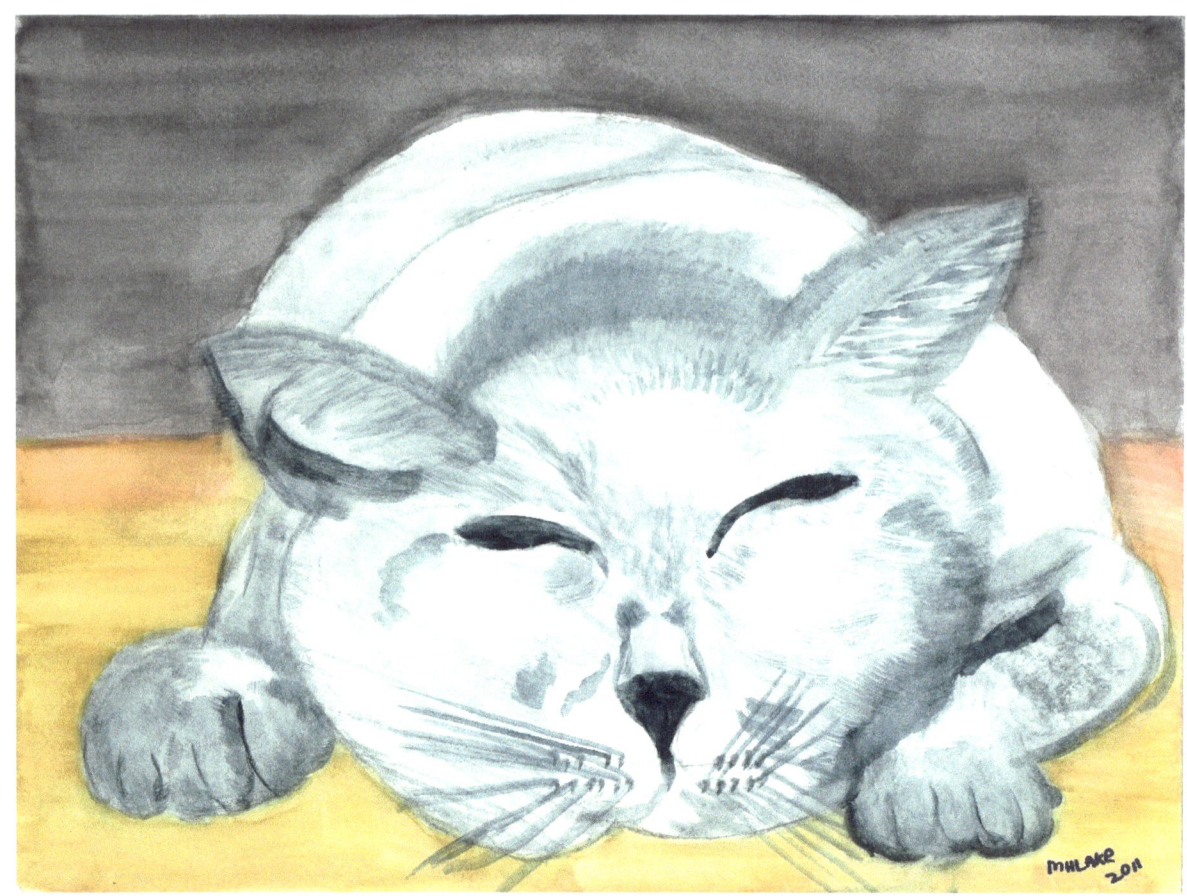

© 2011 MHLAKE

Exercise 9

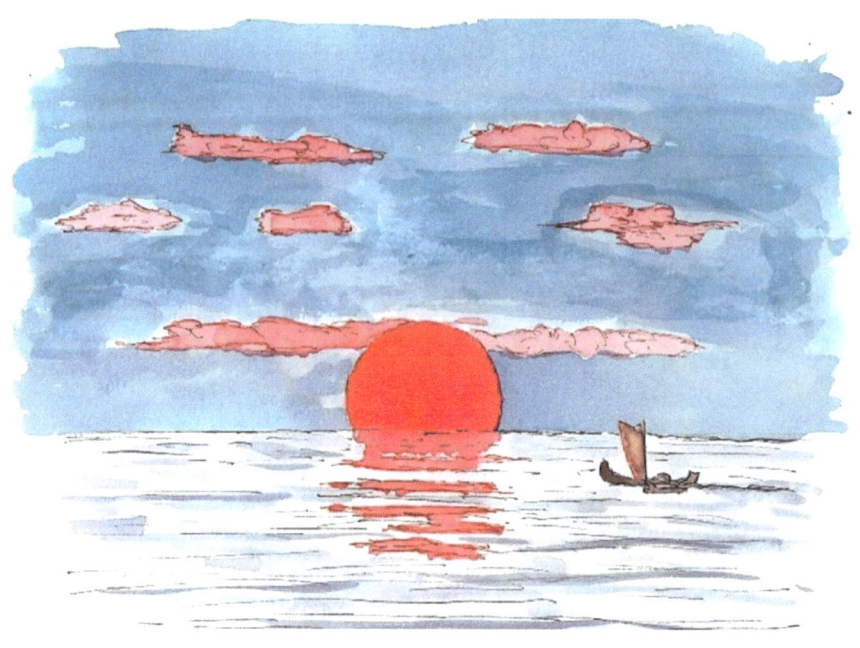

Exercise 10

----

2 PHOTOGRAPHY

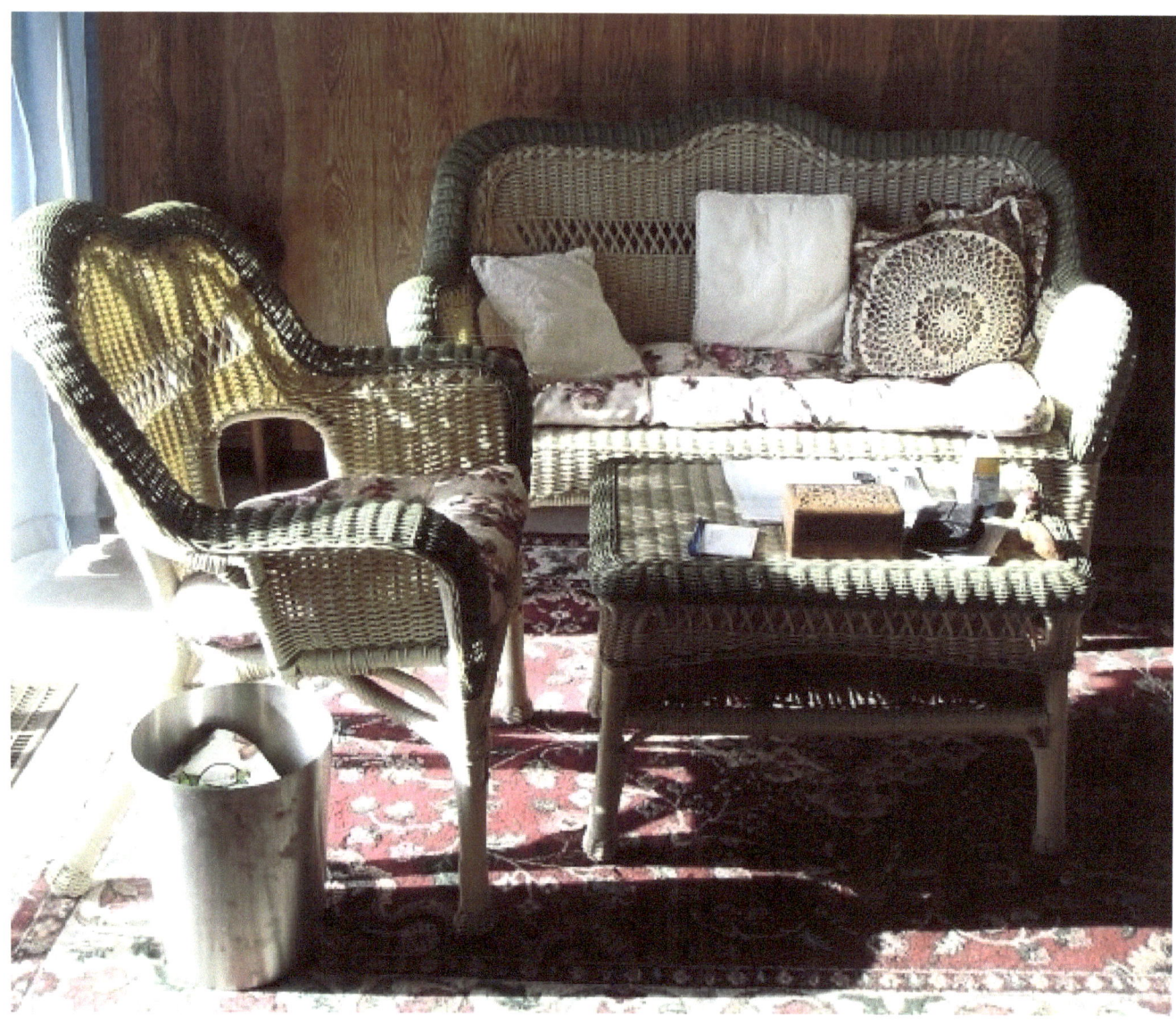

Exercise 11

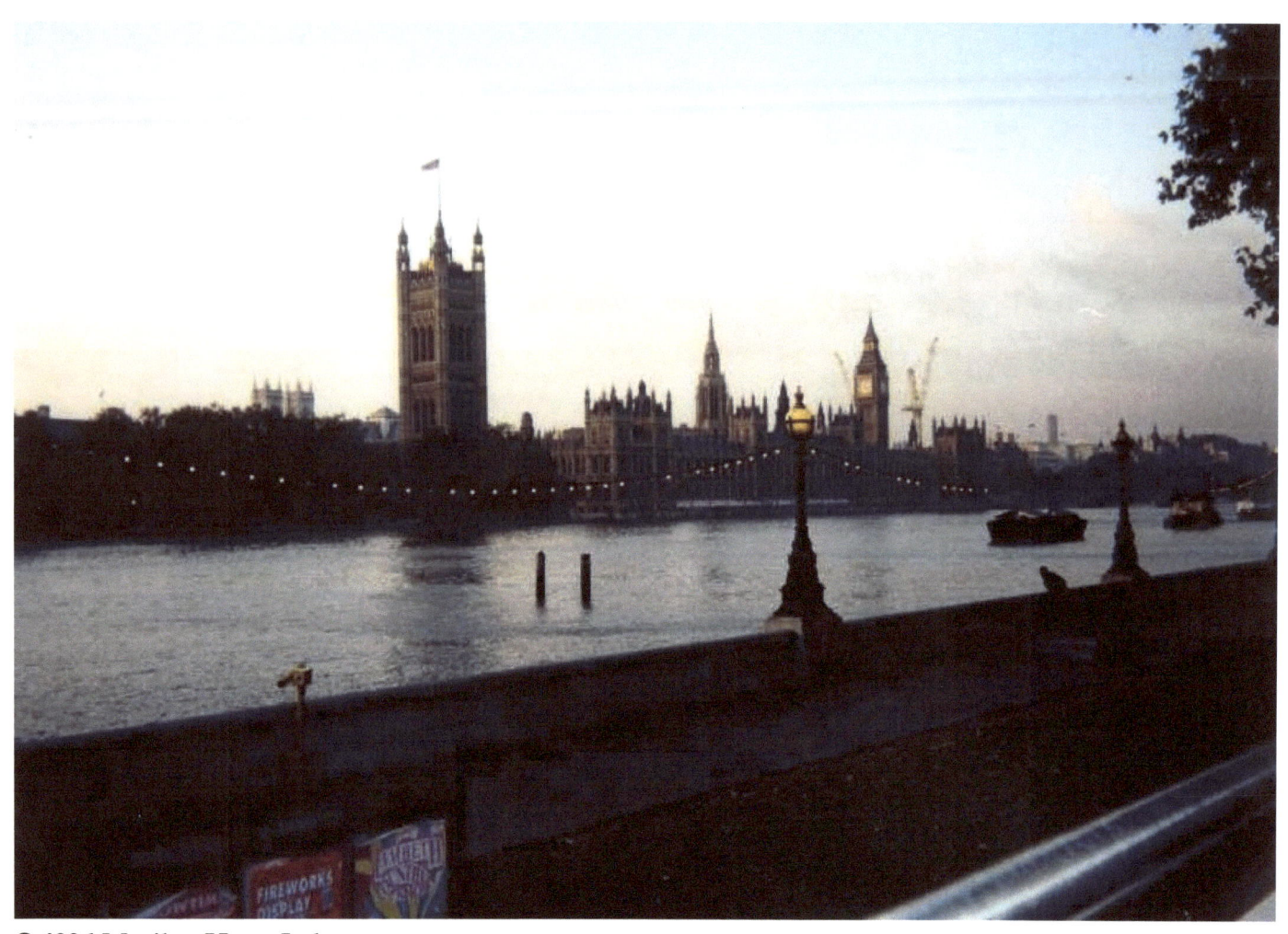

Exercise 12

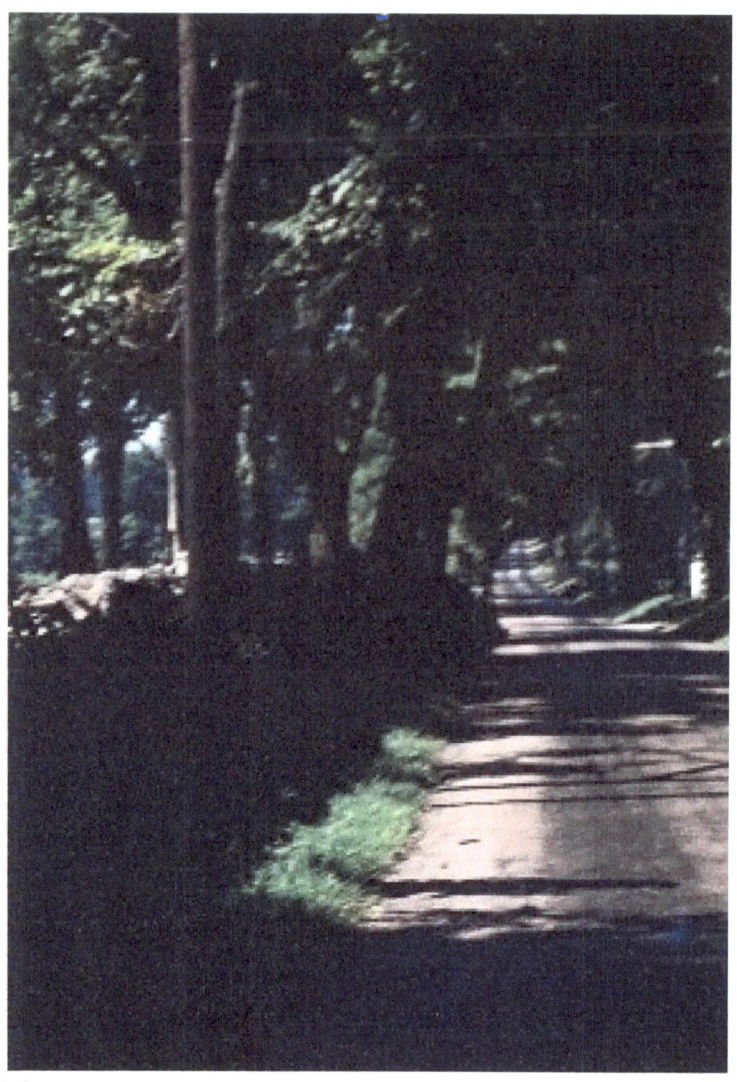

Exercise 13

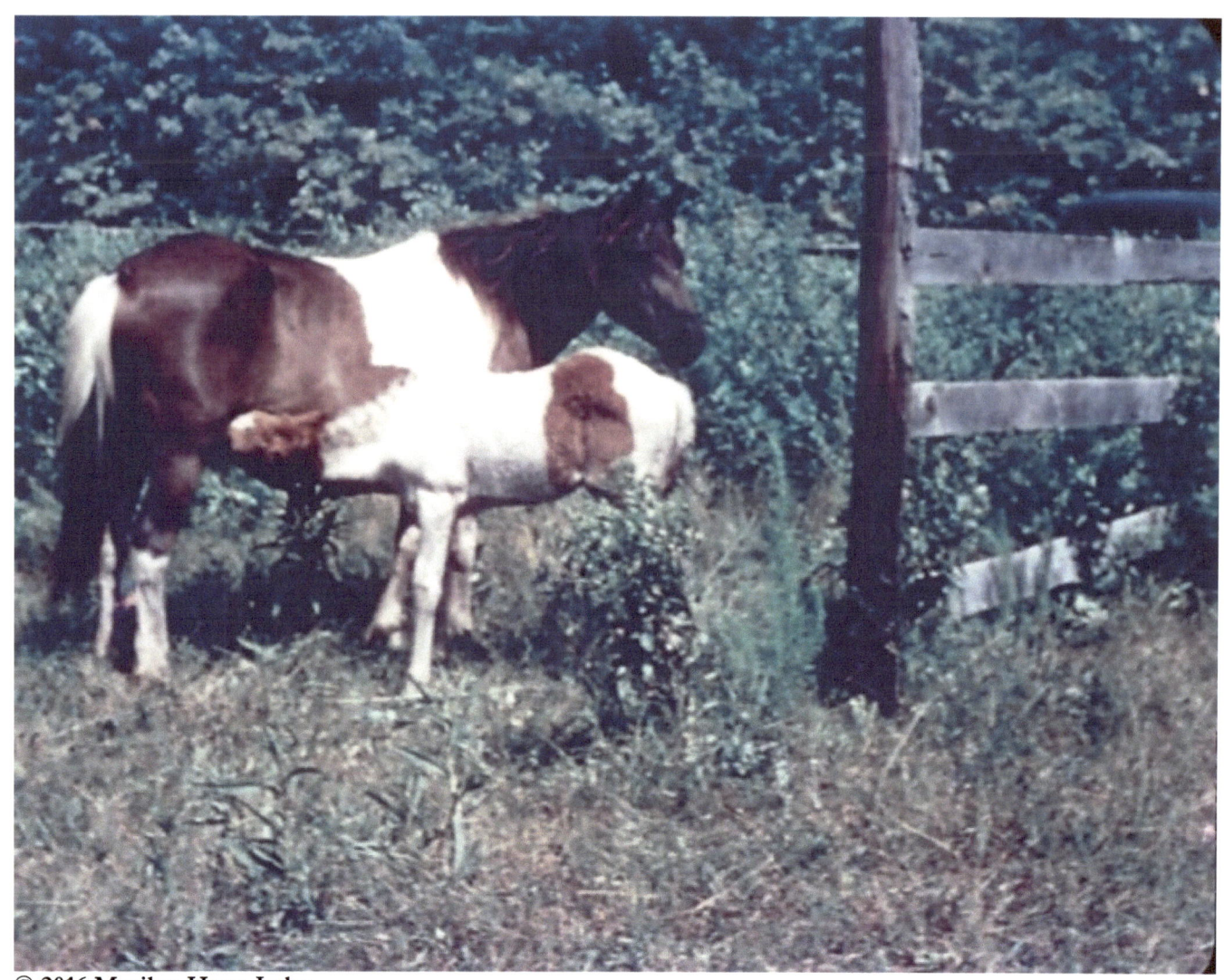

Exercise 14

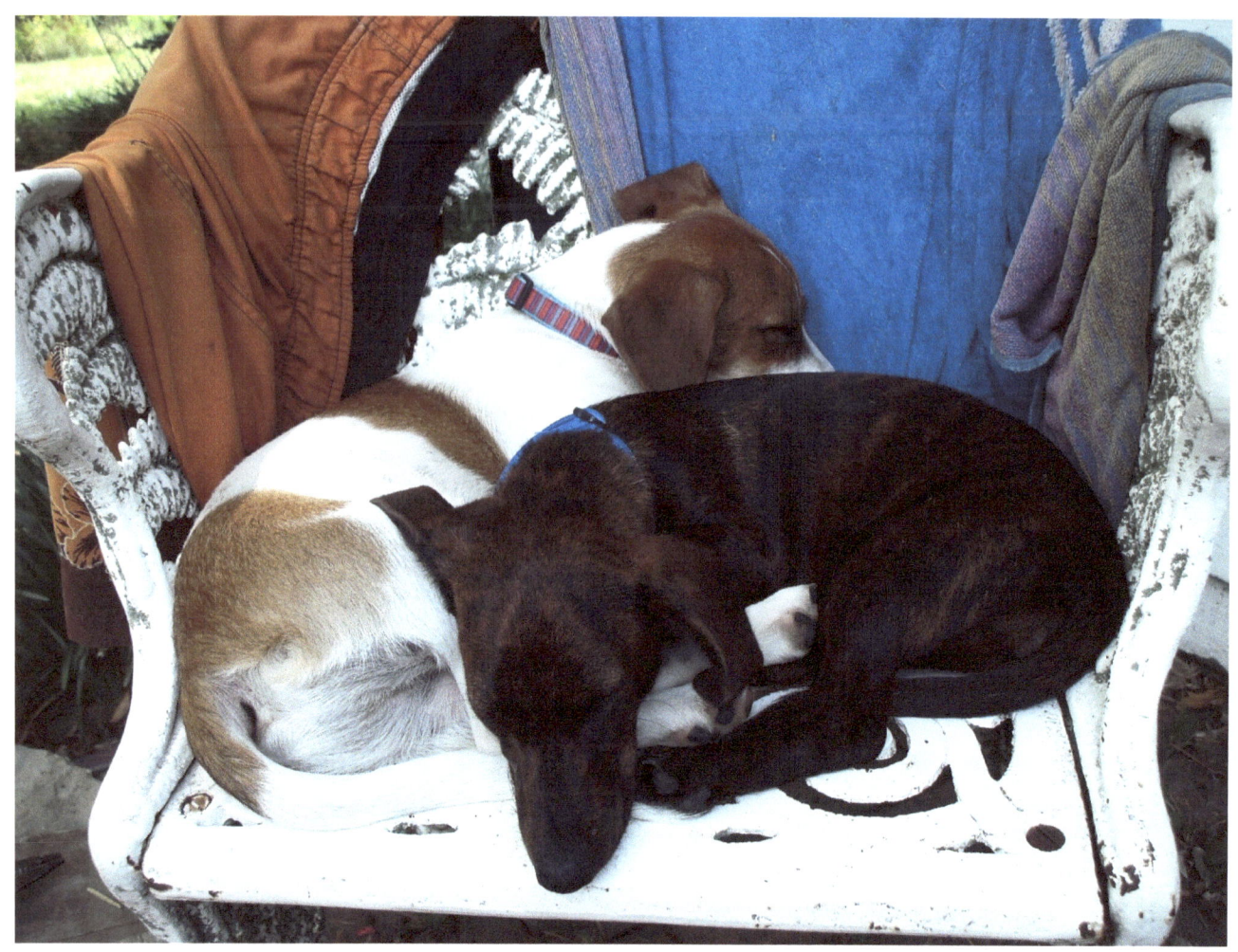

Exercise 15

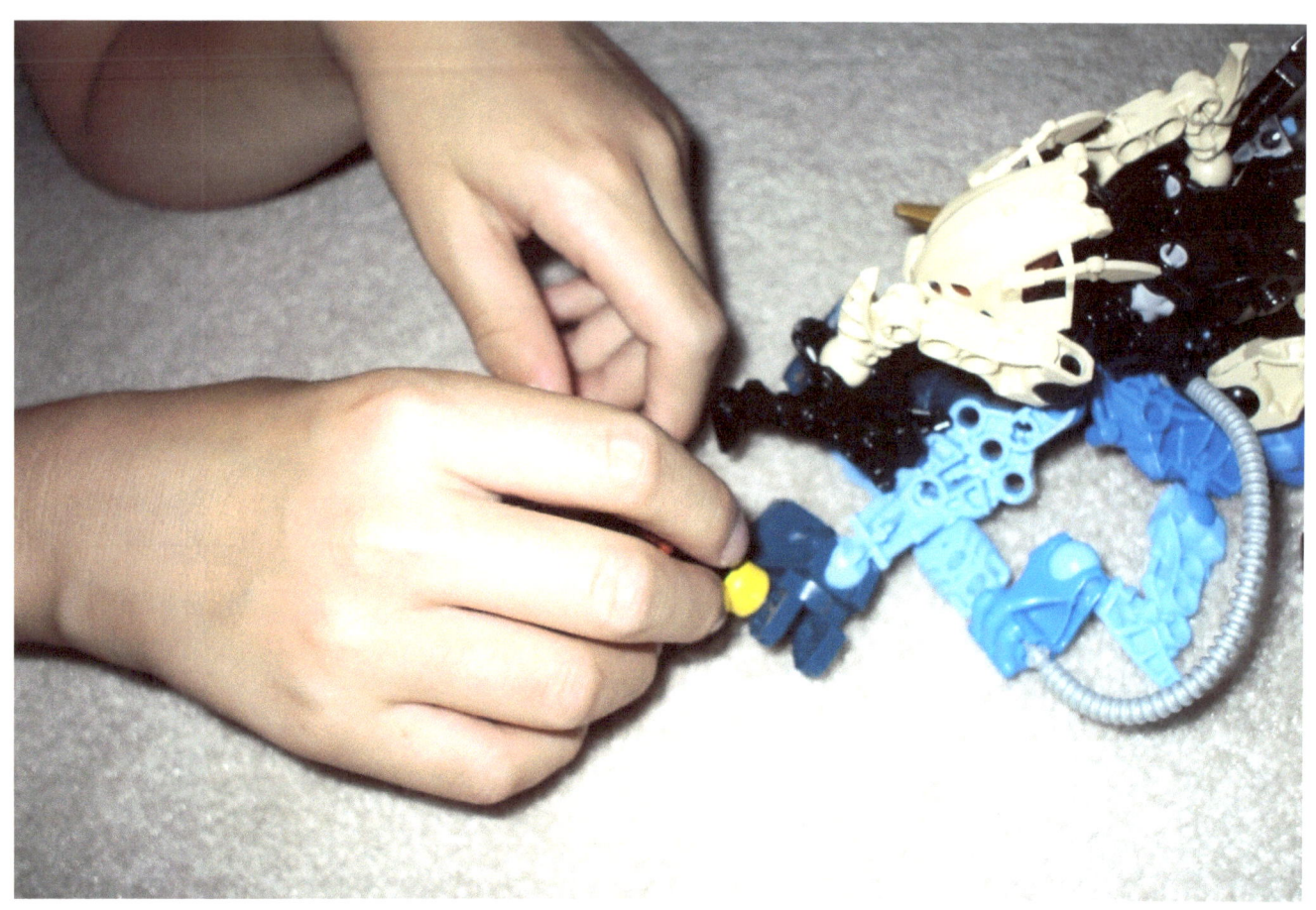

Exercise 16

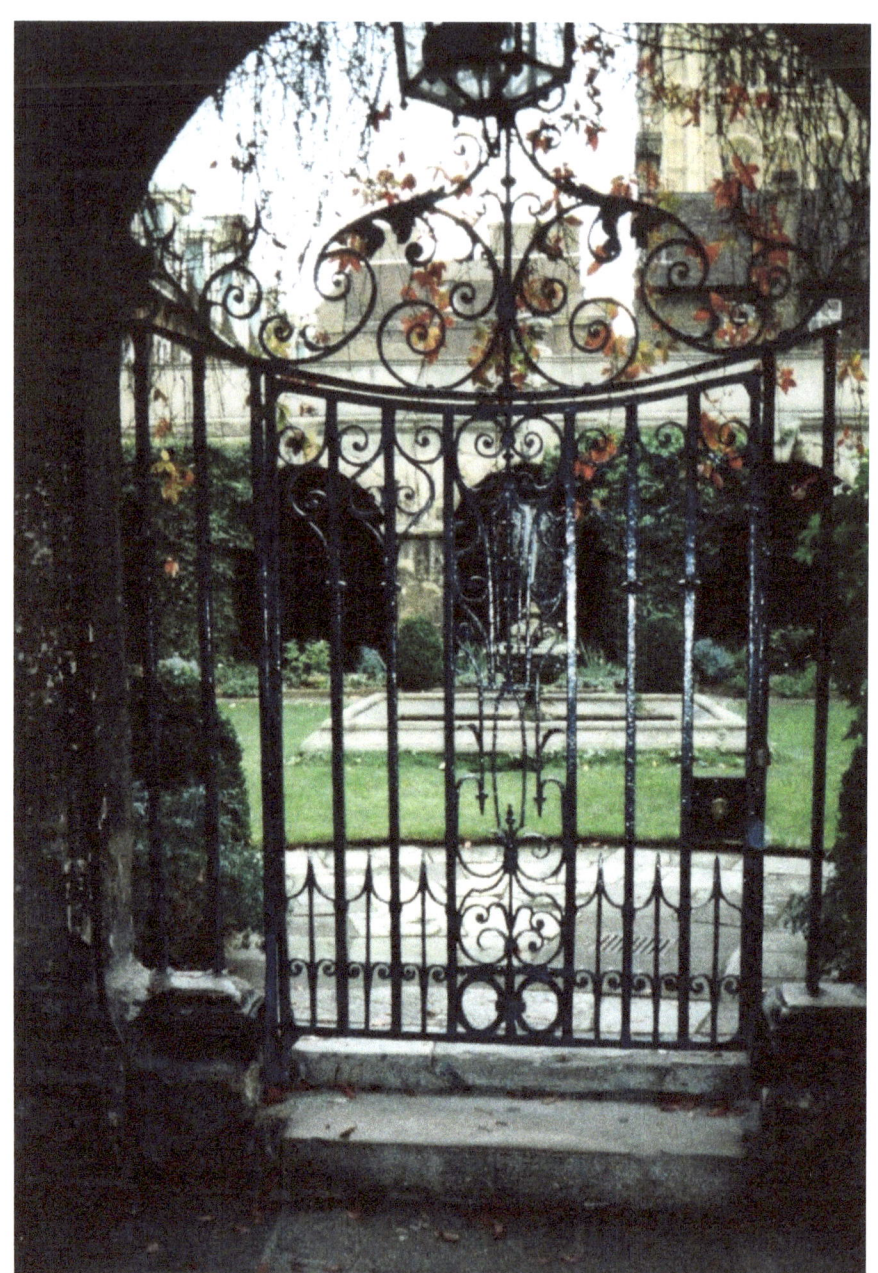

Exercise 17

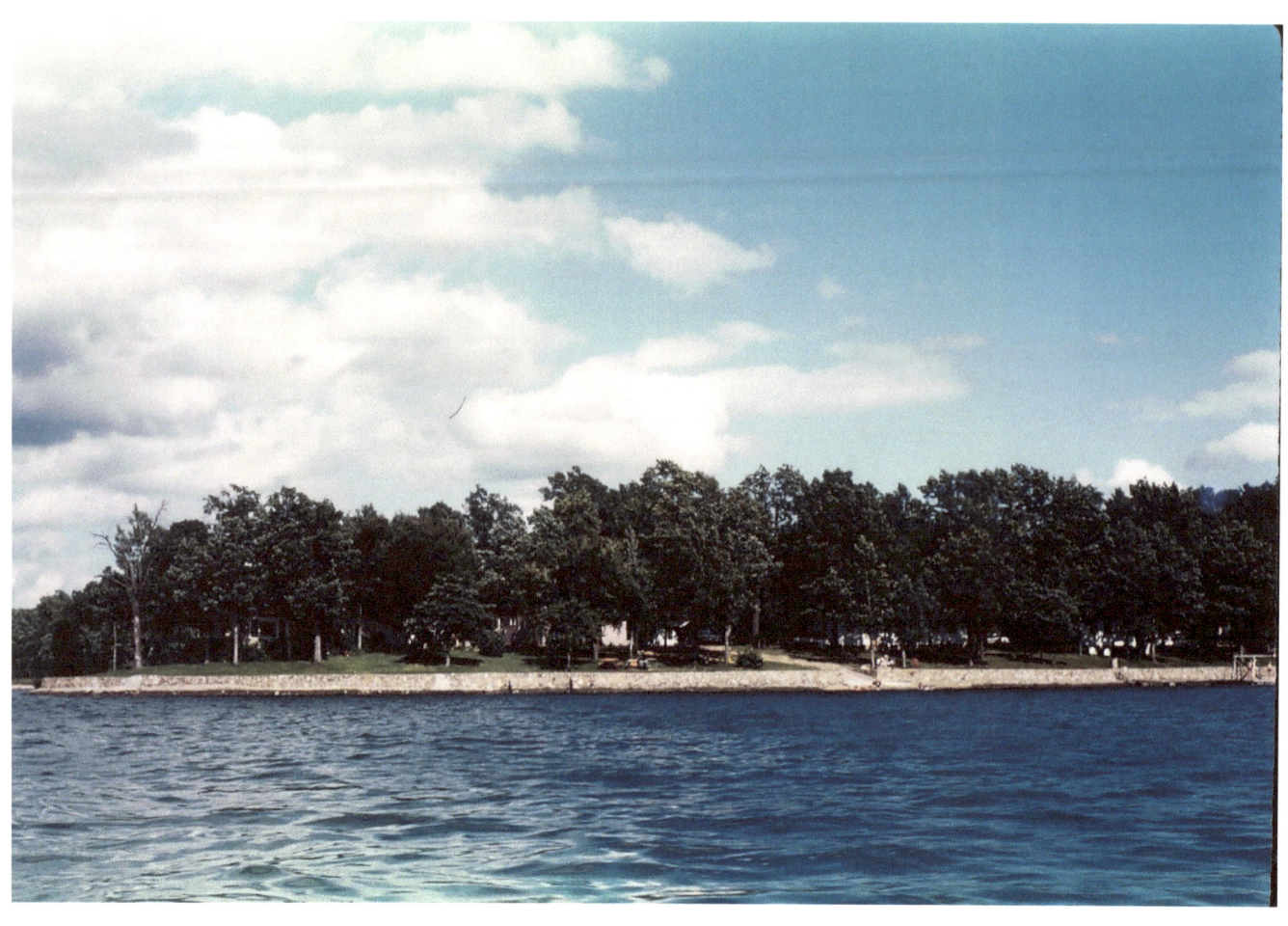

Exercise 18

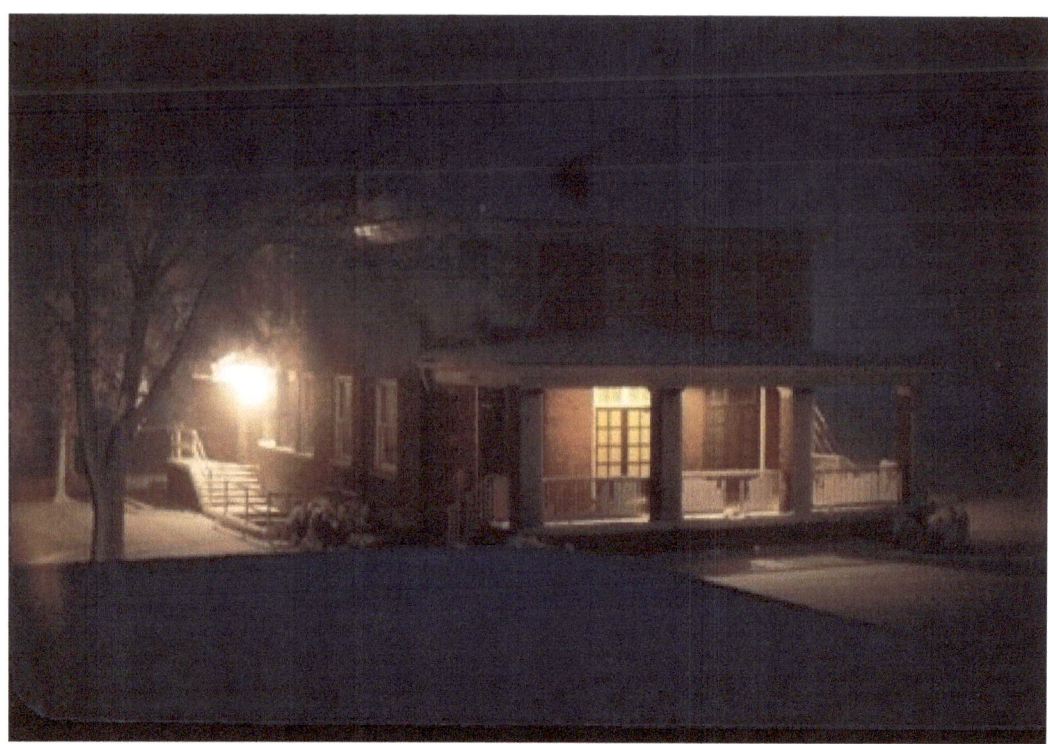

© 1964 Frank J. Waide, Jr.

Exercise 19

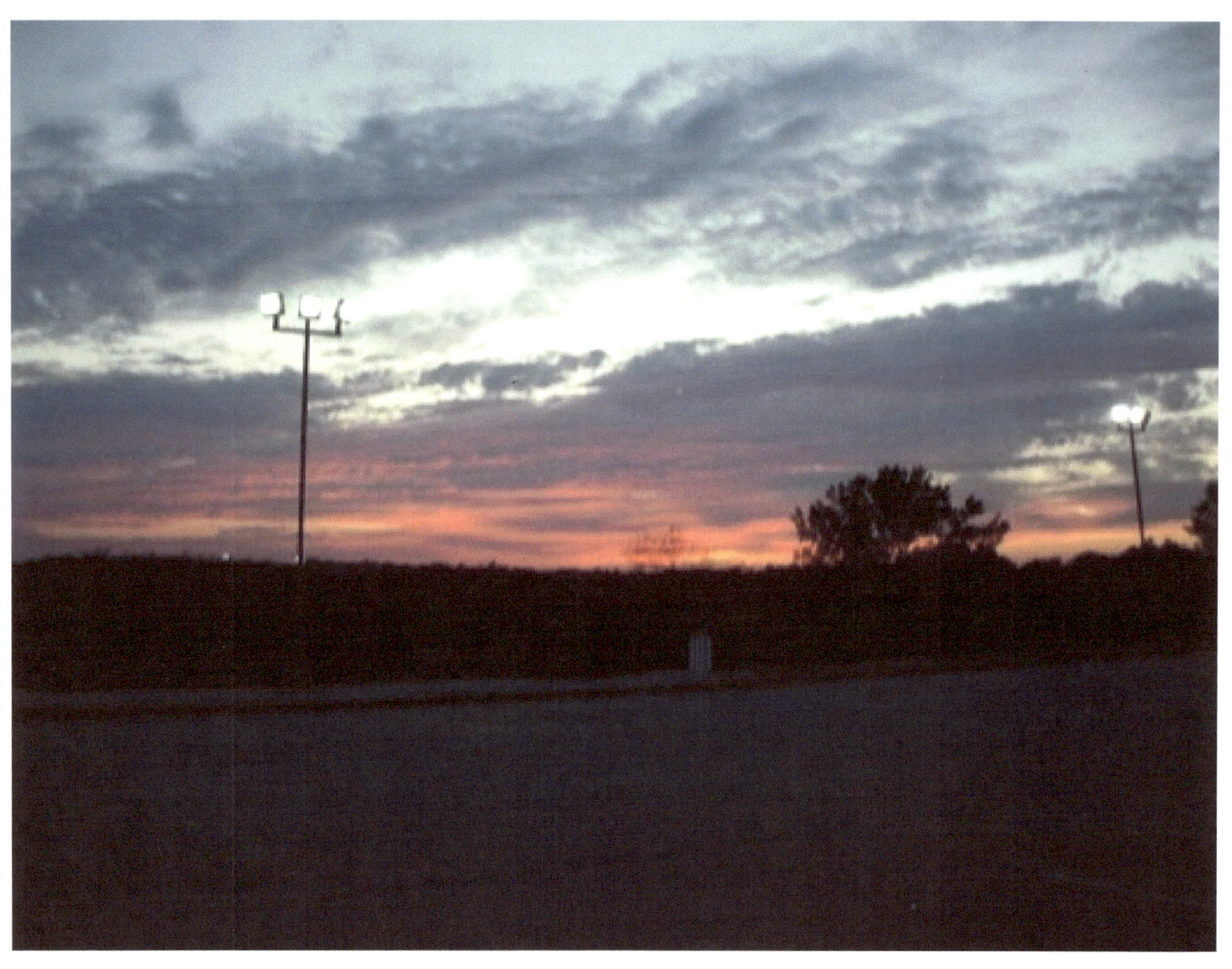

Exercise 20

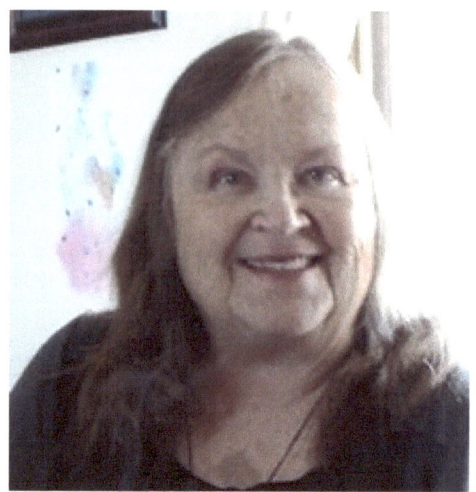

Marilyn Hope Lake, Ph.D., is an award winning painter, and writer, as well as, an amateur photographer. Her love of life, family, friends, nature and God is seen in her work. She resides in Kansas with her husband/illustrator, Denton Warn and two canine companions.

A VERY SPECIAL

THANKS TO

DENTON WARN

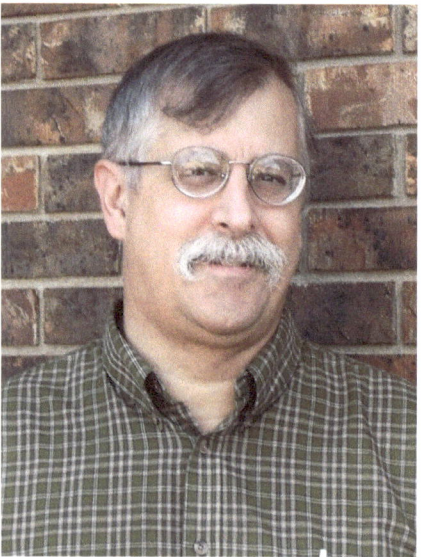

FOR HIS BEAUTIFUL

PEN, INK AND

WATERCOLOR ART

Denton Warn is a surgical technologist and some times illustrator who creates his art with a Parker pen and a child's watercolor set.

OTHER TITLES FROM COMPASS ROSE PUBLICATIONS

Available on Amazon.com, Barnes and Noble.com, KindleDirect.com, CreateSpacedirect.com and from Ingram Distributors.

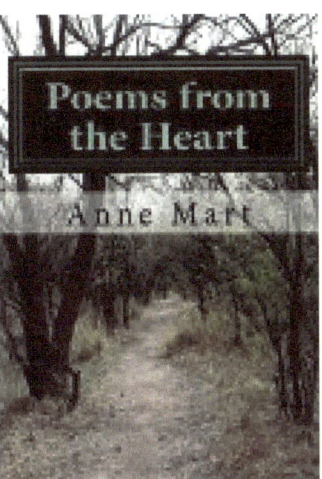

Poems from the Heart: The Collected Poems of Anne Mart, edited by Marilyn Hope Lake. Anne's work takes the most complex of themes and turns them into lyrical, simple lines of poetry that are accessible to persons of all walks of life, status, and education. Anne Mart is a poet of and for her time.

This book contains illustrations by Denton Warn and photography by Deb Hagen of Deb Hagen Photography, KS.

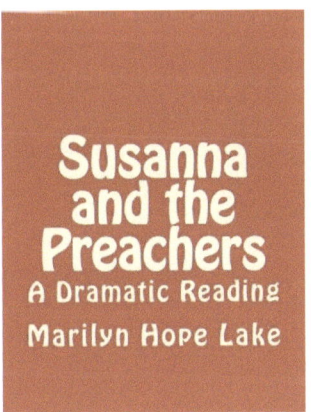

Susanna and the Preachers: A Dramatic Reading by Marilyn Hope Lake. Susanna Wesley was the mother of Charles Wesley who wrote hundreds of Christian hymns and John Wesley who founded the Methodist denomination. Susanna was a woman before her time. She was an independent thinker; she challenged the establishment time and time again. She bore 19 children and raised ten to adulthood, essentially alone. She was a great Christian woman, teacher, survivor and mother. This dramatic reading is designed for simplicity of performance. It can be enhanced; but can be given with minimal costuming and staging. The reading takes approximately 45 minutes as is.

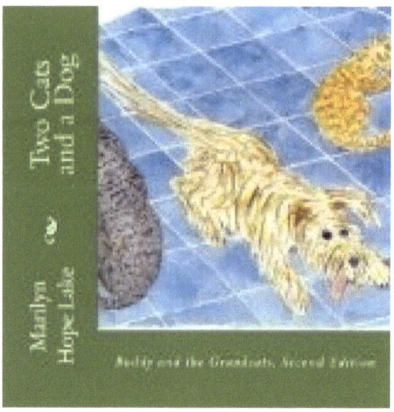

Two Cats and a Dog: Buddy and the Grandcats, 2nd edition, by Marilyn Hope Lake is the charming story of an adult terrier whose home is "invaded by not one, but two adult cats. With insight and humor, the author and illustrator explore the issue of "blended" families. Children and adults alike will delight in the illustrations and learn from Buddy's experience as he discovers how to live peacefully with new additions to his family.

This book has 28 original watercolor illustrations by Denton Warn

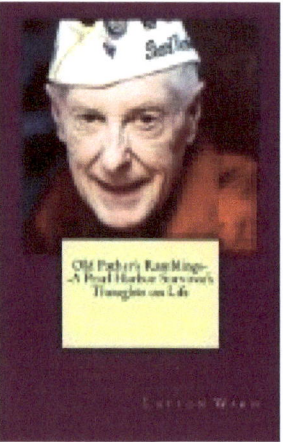

Old Father's Ramblings: A Pearl Harbor Survivor's Thoughts on Life, by Layton Warn, edited by Marilyn Hope Lake. Ninety year-old Layton Warn's book is comprised not only of his touching personal memoirs about the attack on Pearl Harbor December 7, 1941, and his subsequent life in the army stateside; but also of his essays written later in life on the many topics that interested this intelligent and well-read man.. You will be surprised by his unique solutions to problems like the influx of illegal aliens or global warming.

ANOTHER TITLE ILLUSTRATED BY DENTON WARN
Available on Amazon.com and CreateSpacedirect.com

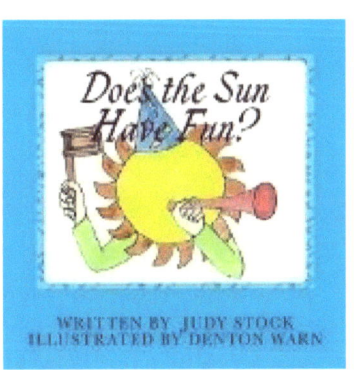

Does the Sun Have Fun ? by Judy Stock has 17 original watercolor illustrations by Denton Warn. This is a charming point of view on what the Sun does when it goes down in the evening. A movie? A pizza? Playing games in the park with its friends? The Sun has many things it can do for fun once it has completed its day's work in the sky.